MW01114529

How to...

Make More Money

in Your Trucking Business

275 Tips from Industry Insiders

Geoffrey R Vautier

CEO, Geoff Vautier International

Copyright © Geoffrey R Vautier, 2015

Print ISBN-13: 978-1507774571

Print ISBN-10: 1507774575

All rights reserved. No part of this publication may be reproduced or distributed in any form or by any means without the prior permission of the author and / or publisher.

The material in this book is provided for educational purposes only. No responsibility for loss occasioned to any person or corporate body acting or refraining to act as a result of reading material in this book can be accepted by the author or publisher.

Interior formatting, cover design and publishing assistance by LOTONtech (www.lotontech.com).

Contents

4

Introduction

The trucking industry is truly amazing. From the clothes we wear to the food we eat and even the gas that fuels our own vehicles, trucking affects literally every part of the economy. Mostly it is invisible, and yet it is there right before our eyes. Trucks going about their business on every road in the country are so commonplace that we often take them for granted, like the buzz of a giant mosquito we choose to ignore.

On average, it is a tough industry — report after report talks about how poor the returns on capital, manpower, resources, fuel and time invested are. Yet, when you dig into the detail, which just happens to be my speciality, you find that there are some companies doing very well, and some doing very poorly.

When it comes to looking at opportunity, averages aren't very useful. Like any industry, trucking provides opportunity for those who work smarter and harder to succeed despite what "averages" might have to say about ROI and earnings potential.

The opportunity I'm talking about is the fact that there is always a way to do something better, with more innovation, creativity and inventiveness. The challenge, of course, is to look outside what we currently know and extend ourselves in ways that might be a smidge outside our current comfort zones.

Here's an analogy that I want to share with you: imagine you are in your seat on a train looking out the window. All you can see is what is shaped by the window, looking out sideways at the passing vista. You have no idea what is coming next and cannot see behind you at what has just passed. The person sitting on the other side of the carriage sees a completely different picture, but still limited within the context of their own window seat. All up and down the train, the story is the same: individual passengers can only see a limited field of vision, dictated by their own "window seats". Now imagine you are the train driver. The view is quite different – you see the horizon on all sides, what you've just left behind in the rear-view mirror and, more importantly, you can see what is coming.

The point of this story is to challenge you to quit being a passenger and become the train driver instead. It easy to fall into the belief that the only view of the world is the one we currently see out the window. But what if we broaden the window? Or, even better, what if we move up to the front of the train and see what's coming before everybody else does?

With that theory in mind, this book is the result of information discussed at workshops held at the New Zealand Road Transport Forum Conference held July 18th through the 20th, in 2014.

The workshops were entitled **"How to increase profits"** in our industry.

My approach was a bit different from how many people would address the issue. If you Google something like "How to increase profits in the trucking industry" or similar terms such as "profitability in the trucking industry," the overwhelming response (greater than 95%, it would seem) will be focused on saving costs: fuel management, driver management, and so forth and so on.

Rather, my view was to consider how we make a bigger pie and, to accomplish that feat, I chose to look at the income side of the business. Not by simply adding new capacity (as many trucking companies invariably do), but in using the existing resources already present in the business, extra revenue has a large impact on the bottom line.

My logic is also based on the following screen shot from the event:

Leverage

	$		
Sales	1,280,000		2.5%
Fuel	240,000	or	13.3%
RUC	176,000	or	Impossible
Repairs	96,000	or	33.3%
Tyres	40,000	or	80.0%
Wages	300,000	or	10.6%
Depreciation	172,000	or	Impossible
Overhead / finance	224,000	or	13.3%
Profit (2.5%)	32,000		
Want to double your profit?			32,000

In this example, we have a mythical – but quite typical – trucking business to use as a case study. It makes a small profit – about 2.5% on turnover. The question is, "If we wanted to double the annual profit, what exactly would it require?"

In this case, that would equate to an "on the books" improvement of $32,000. The percentages in the right hand column show how much the underlying cost or revenue would have to change to achieve that specific goal. Most people focus on the cost side of the equation, and yet the item with the greatest leverage is sales.

Imagine this hypothetical conversation: we call our drivers into the office and say the business needs to improve and "we need a 10.6% drop in your pay packets". Or we talk to the customer and say "we need a 2.5% rate increase". I think we'd all agree that the latter conversation is probably the easier one to have!!! (Though, naturally, neither is particularly "easy".)

And in many cases, increasing revenue is not necessarily a price increase matter. Line items like improved efficiency and/or better loads also do the trick. The point is that we often overlook the easy stuff and focus on the hard stuff instead. I called it leverage; gaining momentum by thinking outside the box, doing things differently or simply more effectively.

For instance, a small percentage increase onto the total sales line is the same as a big percentage on *one* of the lines. Opening yourself to new ideas, stretching your comfort zone and working through different scenarios are all valid examples of using leverage to your advantage. This book is designed to get you thinking about how to focus on the revenue side of the business and use that leverage to increase profits in the trucking industry.

The format of the workshop I mentioned earlier was a series of seven leading questions covering different aspects of the trucking business. Participants worked in groups of five to seven individuals to discuss the question. They then reported their answers/solutions to the wider group at large.

The notes that follow are bullet point answers to those questions, some of which I've expounded on when necessary to clarify a point or speak to a larger issue. The intention of this book's unique format is simply to create memory joggers, to sow little seeds of ideas that might resonate with you. The majority of them will hopefully set you thinking about an issue in a way – or possibly even *ways* – that you hadn't thought of before. These are ideas generated by your fellow truckies, so they are real, proven and current. Some may be contradictory – that's fine as well. What is life if not a little bumpy, and how are we to learn if we're never pushed to consider the other side of an issue – even one we think we know "everything" about?

As you read these the ideas, instead of shaking your head and saying "I can't do that," stop and think about the underlying logic to the idea and consider the possibility that "just maybe I *could* do that".

There are over 275 ideas – some will work for you. Even if it's only a fraction of them, imagine how much your industry, your business, your attitude and, of course, your profits could improve.

See how you get on, and I'd love to hear which ideas worked best for you. Or if you want further assistance, I'm happy to discuss them with you. Either way, my contact information is below.

Geoff Vautier

January 2015

+64 212 459014

geoff@howtoincreaseprices.com

Question 1

What value do you provide to the customer?

What Value Do You Provide to the Customer?

The purpose of this question is to get you to think about what it is that you do for clients, how well you do it and, additionally, what might constitute "value" to the clients you serve.

Before you answer, let's make sure we're on the same page as far as "value" is concerned. Basically, **Value** is the entire package of benefits that a client gets from dealing with you:

- The job that is actually done;

- The service that comes with it;

- The way they are treated as customers;

- How they are dealt with by the drivers;

- The quality of the job, how they are made to feel;

- Their experience in dealing with you as a supplier;

As you can see, there are a wide range of possibilities on this list. All of these ideas represent potential "value" to the client. Use them to discuss the value you provide, and add your own variables of service or delivery to the list.

This personalization of service, product and delivery becomes what we refer to as your "value proposition". Think of the value proposition in terms of, "This is what we do for you and it crates value to you because **fill in the blank here**."

Remember that clients understand value; what it looks like to them, what they expect, what they need and how much that means to them. And when they *do* understand it, they are prepared to pay for it. Identifying and explaining that value can be the basis of charging higher prices, and making greater profits.

The other key in describing value is to first understand what is important to that particular client. In other words, every client will define value differently, based on his or her own wants, needs, even budget.

While your overall service is important, there will be some things that are *really* important to a specific client, for a specific reason(s). For example, it may be timeliness, because the client's processes depend on things happening in a specific order. In other cases, it might be that the product is perishable so that temperature control is important. In yet others it might be product handling.

How to Provide Service to the Customer

Once you know what is important to each client, personally tailor your service to focus on those aspects and make the case that there is a premium for addressing that need in a most specific way.

To that end, here are a variety ways in which you can provide value to customers:

Take their problems away

All business is essentially about removing problems from the customer's life. The extent to which you can do that effectively increases the perceived value of your service. You are an expert in your business – use that knowledge to solve problems and get paid to do it.

Be flexible to meet changing circumstances

By being adaptable and flexible, you can anticipate problems before they arrive. In other words, solve problems for the client, don't create them.

This also gives you scope to increase what you do for the client, and to charge accordingly. To the extent that you are already on top of the problem, it stops the client from going to the outside market for an alternate solution.

Offer partnerships and joint solutions that share the risks and benefits of collaboration

By involving the client in this process of sharing risks and profits, there are two benefits:

1. The potential outcomes are better because you can set higher goals, knowing that there is limited risk and more resources.
2. You lock the customer into the process and your business, because to walk away means they lose these benefits.

Provide Health and Safety meetings with staff

Health and safety have become major issues these days in all business ventures, across all industries. Given that you will have addressed them in your own business, with a particular focus on, say, materials handling because that is what you do day in and day out, then it is imperative you pass that expertise on to the client as an added value.

Offer a profit share option

Often when pricing, we take all the risk by having sharp prices and not really knowing what is involved. Offering a profit share enables you to share the risk, by charging a fair price while providing an incentive for the customer to get involved and receive benefits if it all works out.

Capitalize on customer empathy

Don't underestimate the value of making the customer feel understood and appreciated. It gives them confidence to trust you and become their preferred supplier.

Provide peace of mind that the job will be done well

Peace of mind is a powerful selling tool. By doing the job in a competent manner and maintaining regular contact with the client, you have the ability to provide the client the assurance that they do not need to worry about the job, and they can focus on other matters.

Identify customized solutions to best satisfy customer compliance and Health and Safety requirements

Using your unique knowledge and skill set(s), you have the ability to identify the best way of approaching the job to make sure it meets the clients expectations and is done in a manner that meets all current Health and Safety requirements.

How to Improve Your Performance

One way to increase profits without incurring debt is to focus on your performance. In other words, what can you do to increase value for the client by enhancing what you already do for them?

Here are a variety of ways to do just that:

Do the job in a reliable way

A basic axiom of business is to do your job in a reliable manner. Word will spread that you can be "trusted" to do the job well, on budget and on time. Reliability is a sign of professionalism, and quickly gains the confidence of the client. That creates a net positive in the relationship and, naturally, is of great value to the client.

Do the job in a consistent way

When you do your job in a consistent manner, it shows professionalism, respect for a job well done and ultimately gains the confidence of the client. This builds customer loyalty and leads to not only repeat business but, as word of mouth spreads, increased business as well.

Provide on-time service

Many clients tend to live by routine, and want their business to run in much the same manner. Either coming or going, transport is often an integral part of their processes. You need to understand punctuality from the client's point of view, and especially what is important to them in terms of due dates and deliverables. In some environments, such as congested cities, it will take extra effort to achieve a stated goal. This is a valuable outcome to the client, and it can be a basis for higher charges.

Be adaptable

While we all like routine, things don't always go as planned. Being adaptable inspires the client and gives them confidence that you pay attention to the details. Done right, adaptability means that you can become a trusted partner in the business and a first port of call. As always, change brings with it opportunity.

Deliver what is promised

Being counted upon to deliver on your promise is a basic tenet of business, and one that is highly valued by virtually all clients. It is also good business practice within your own business, as it encourages standards of quality and excellence, internally and externally. To insure that new and potential clients know of your reliability, get testimonials regarding your past performance and use them to up-sell your business to others.

Follow up on promises and do what you say you will do

It has been said that the best salesmen are those that simply follow up and do what they promise. Making promises creates an expectation with the client, which anyone can do. Delivering on that promise provides the real value, and is something that very few do. When you do, it will build your brand as a consistently reliable transport provider.

Having a "Bring it on" attitude

Undertake your work with urgency, a can-do attitude, and be positive when it comes to your ability to get the job done, regardless of the obstacles. Be a "yes" company, not a "no" company. This attitude naturally inspires confidence and boosts your client's morale. Being a wilting wallflower is not a good look for a "can do" company.

Invest in efficiency of service and speed of response

We live in an age where expectations of service times are rapidly decreasing – it is the "we want it now" generation. Even though it might be tough, embracing this attitude and delivering is highly valuable in a climate of competitors who simply can't rise to the challenge.

Maintain a safety focus, for both you and the client

Safety is a big issue; workplace accidents (deservedly) get too much press, and sophisticated clients know to ask about this. Keeping yourself – as well as your clients – out of the news is a valuable asset in these dangerous times.

How to Make Things Personal

Clients appreciate companies that can provide them with both peak, but also personal, performance. Making the client think you exist only to meet their needs is a great way to give them a personal experience that translates into repeat business.

Maintain a high level of communication

Keep the lines of communication open. Communication provides reassurance that the process is working. Never underestimate the value that this trait provides for the client, particularly confidence that the job is being done right.

Establish relationships with the key players so they feel free to raise issues with you

The age of personal contact has not passed! In fact, it may be more valued than ever. Having a situation where the client feels able to raise issues is a big positive in not only fostering communication, but also confidence.

Be confident in your ability and delivery of the service

You are the expert; never forget that. People like dealing with experts. Being confident in your abilities inspires the client, and rubs off on their business.

Enhance your reputation in the public arena on behalf of the client

In many situations, you are the face of the client. From small items such as the presentation of your vehicle, to the attitude of your drivers, to the condition in which the load arrives, all of this reflects back onto your client. The customer to whom you are delivering also sees you as extension of your client. You play a pivotal role in enhancing the reputation of your client, which is not to be taken lightly.

Be approachable and accessible

Most businesses are a people thing. No matter how big the organization, it is essentially people dealing with people. Being approachable and accessible shows you care, and that won't go unnoticed by your customers.

Be available for questions

Issues always crop up, inevitably, and if not dealt with promptly and transparently can cause doubt and concern. Encouraging questions from your clients is a positive initiative to engage in before, during and after the sale of your transport services.

Be proactive in proposing solutions and anticipating situations that need addressing

You have a unique perspective on the client's business. You also have specialist-level knowledge on matters that they might either know very little about, or indeed care greatly about. Nevertheless, the issues rarely go away by themselves. Your insights are valuable in terms of proposing solutions and anticipating situations that need addressing.

Have face-to-face contact

People like to deal with people; actual people. In ever business, in every industry, it simply makes the world go round. Since this is an increasingly rare commodity, the more you do it, the more valuable you become to your customers.

Know the customers' business and be able to deliver the service without having to constantly refer back to them

When you are in tune with the customer's business, you often have the ability to solve problems without having to refer back to the client for constant direction. This saves them time, and means they don't have to divert their attention on a regular basis, making it an extremely valuable skill set.

Discuss the ever growing compliance requirements and about the customer themselves

Health, safety and general compliance with legal matters is a factor of the modern business world. You are well placed in your area of expertise to advise the clients on what such issues mean, a fact they will be most grateful for. Being proactive will be of value to them, and enhances your reputation.

Offer competitive pricing and value for the money

All businesses are looking to save costs on a regular basis. Competitive pricing and value for money are not mutually exclusive. It is a matter of explaining what that value is in way that is plain and actionable to the client.

Enhance Your Skill Set(s)

Clients want skilled service providers, and are willing to pay a higher premium for those that exemplify the skill sets they require.

Provide specialized skills and business expertise

It is highly likely that you provide specialized skills, particularly compared to the client. This can be in a whole range of areas, from driving the trucks to logistics planning to understanding general business conditions in your locality to understanding events further afield to what's happening in other types of businesses. Every one of these skills and sub-sets adds value to you as a transport provider.

Act with safety, quality and professionalism in mind

By adopting a safety ethos, which is already a legal requirement, you tend to automatically up the performance levels across your whole business.

Have product expertise and use the right equipment

Never forget that, when it comes to transport, you are the expert in doing what you do. One of the benefits is that you have the ability to recommend and use the right equipment for the job. Ultimately, this is to everyone's benefit.

Enhance Your Product Line

The products you offer – or don't offer – are likely to make or break your appeal to a prospective customer. To ensure that you are always at your most attractive, enhance as well as promote your product line to attract new customers and increase profit.

Use your buying power to create leverage

It is likely that your business has significant buying power for goods and services in your area of expertise. For example, storage. In any event, there may be avenues where these can be used to benefit the client.

Target the products that specifically meet the client's needs

It is likely that within your business there are many strands, and options, that will specifically meet a customer's needs in ways that are unique to them. You can add value by first understanding the client's needs, and then choosing the best product fit to meet that need. If it is a potentially valuable contract, then consider customizing the product.

Provide end-to-end solutions

In the vein of adding value, if you can add end-to-end solutions that encompass the job from start to finish – and often above the call of duty – it is both valuable to the client and makes it harder for other people to wrestle the contract away from you.

Provide a point of difference

A point of difference can add value and make you unique, so that it is very difficult to compare offerings with other parties (should you be in a competitive situation). Also, the stronger the point of difference, the more likely that you are offering something that others may not be able to provide.

Promote their name through sign writing on your truck

If public recognition is important to the client, then an option to become a mobile billboard for them could be very valuable. Now more than ever, with magnetic signs or even affordable, temporary painting, this is a likely and attractive added value product/service.

Undertake a job safety assessment / discussion

Turn your expertise in health and safety into a product that can be sold to other businesses.

Use your knowledge to provide better solutions than they might come up with

Use your expertise in your specialist field to come up with solutions that are appealing to the client. After all, you live and breathe transportation 24/7 whereas it is only a sideline to them.

Upgrade Your Equipment

Upgrading your equipment can be costly, but it doesn't have to break the bank. When you consider it an investment in future earnings, you will also feel more comfortable sharing such upgrades with clients, who are likely to appreciate that you'll be transporting their goods in the latest style, efficiency and, of course, safety.

Invest in whole-of-life trucks

By making an investment in the whole-of-life of a truck – from point of purchase to upkeep, warranty and maintenance through the truck's sale/re-sale after a specific amount of time – you ensure increased profitability by less time off the road due to maintenance and upkeep.

Lower your costs by adopting new technologies

Inevitably technology continues its relentless march forward, leaving outdated and less valuable companies in its wake. This should be embraced, not feared. New technologies such as tire inflation, shock-less suspensions, and bearing monitoring will ultimately help lower costs and improve efficiency on and off the road. These cost savings can be shared with the client in terms of lower fees for your service(s). The operative word is "share" – the tradition has been to give most of these benefits away.

Provide specialized equipment

By definition, this equipment will enable you to perform better, achieve more and give you a capability to do things you couldn't do before. It's all added value to the client, thus a good investment for you. The advantage you have is that you can share the costs amongst many clients over time, thus recouping your investment in a timely manner.

Use products that are reliable and thus minimizes downtime issues for the client

It goes without saying that minimal downtime and reliability benefits everyone.

Invest in high quality equipment

The adage is that quality is remembered long after the price is forgotten. On average, good quality gear allows you to perform at a higher standard.

Maintain equipment so that it is always in top condition

Value always comes back to reliability. The old adage here is that a small amount of prevention far outweighs spending a heap of time and money on a "cure". Maintaining your equipment is yet another cog in the wheel of providing a reliable service.

Maintain a high standard of cleanliness and appearance of your equipment

Clean, routinely maintained and modern equipment is a discipline that tends to work its way into the ethos of the rest of the business. It may be a small item, but it is important to the client – and your own staff.

Question 2:

How Do You Increase Revenue in Your Existing Business?

Question 2

How Do You Increase Revenue in Your Existing Business?

The purpose of this question is to help you understand how you can increase revenue from your existing asset base (and make more profits), rather than simply buying another asset, which seems to be a favored approach in this industry and yet one with a diminishing rate of return.

Doubling up on a poorly run business is not a smart way to achieve success, while the following ideas are.

Prices and Products

What are you currently charging versus what you are currently offering, product-wise? Are there ways to increase the value of what you have, simply by re-labelling it or refocusing it? That is the focus of the following ideas:

Rate increases that can be justified

This is an example of low hanging fruit. The key is to justify the increase in price with logic, and explaining the value that you provide. See the previous question for some of the many ways you can provide value to a client, many of which you already probably do.

Identify specialist skills / equipment that are only being charged out at normal rates and increase the charges

Don't underrate – or undersell – your experience and the skills of your staff. It is natural to gain experience as the business grows, and unnatural not to capitalize on that experience with increased fees. A cost-plus mentality often leads us to undervalue what it is that we actually provide. Identify those skills and equipment, and consider whether you are retaining enough of the value.

Don't underrate – or undersell – the skill that you have

Never forget, the ability to manage multiple issues and get a result is a valuable skill. Managing a diverse business with lots of moving parts is also a difficult task. Unfortunately, just because *we* think something is simple (because we do it all the time), we assume that is the case for everybody else as well. Often, however, it is not. Trust that fact and bill accordingly.

Charge for added value services, such as those identified in the prior question

In Question 1, we identified many types of value that the client receives. Many of them are incidental to what we physically do, yet their value is very tangible, particularly to the customer. Consider ways that you can charge for those benefits.

Expand the product range

Even though your business is essentially "moving stuff," think of your business as a series of products and services. There may be add-ons and items that you do for one customer that could become something you can offer other customers. Continually assess and re-assess how to "bundle," or at least "broadcast," those items into added value – and increased profit.

Charge out labor where the waiting time is over and beyond what was agreed to as a result of the client's actions/inaction

When new contracts are negotiated, the rosy picture is always presented. The client is always ready for the pickup, the staff is always on call, and no one is ever late or falls behind. In reality, of course, that is not always the case. When you negotiate a contract, set these activities out as things the client undertakes to do. If they don't perform, then consider charging for cost and manpower overruns. The true cost of having a driver idle is not just the lost wages, but the lost opportunity of using that truck and driver on another, income-earning project. Don't absorb that cost alone if you don't have to, particularly if it was the client's fault.

Charge for incidentals

We tend to think of incidental costs as part of the business, but with a well-structured contract some of these should be passed back to the client.

Implement regular rate increases

Have a series of small increases over time is easier to accept than massive increases at random intervals simply because you need a cash infusion.

Effective Use of Assets and People

Oftentimes we can increase profits simply by using the assets, resources, people and time we have more effectively:

Improve the productivity of your people

Productivity, time management and your staff is an age-old issue, but more and more it is the case that there are tools that can help. Now more than ever, these range from technology that helps them do their jobs better (e.g. scanning / iPad) to technology that makes sure they are doing what they are supposed to be doing, i.e. time trackers and the like. An investment in either can result in a more effective use of your assets and people, resulting in increased profits.

Identify partnerships with other "truckies" to eliminate empty running

Now more than ever there appears to be a willingness to co-operate with what are essentially your competitors. And why not? After all, it makes no sense for three trucks to drive down the same road with partial loads when one truck with a full load would do the job much more efficiently. There are many ways to make this work, from clipping the ticket to alternating the work to doing different parts of the job.

Conduct operational reviews to assess your performance against best practices

It is easy to be mesmerised by the rosy view that you see from your office window, and believe that is your whole reality. (For reference, refer to the train story in the introduction). Challenging yourself to be measured against best practices takes a lot of guts, but the payoff can be significant in terms of ROI. The research suggests that there is a significant difference between the best and worst performers, which means, for most people, there is (always) room to improve. Those improvements can translate to added value for the customer, and more profits in your pocket.

Know what you can target to improve efficiencies

By thoroughly understanding the business and the numbers as they exist in reality, you will quickly get a good understanding as to where there is room to improve. Increasing efficiency has the same bottom line effect as increasing revenue.

Target driver behaviors / driving habits

Monitoring driving behaviours, habits and possible ways to improve efficiency will go a long way toward making the most use of your and your driver's time. Now more than ever, there is technology that allows this to be monitored. Make use of it, and thank me later!

Utilize your truck assets better

Ask yourself whether your trucks are being productive all the time. In many cases, there will be slippage – servicing being done during work hours, trucks held on jobs because of client delays, etc. In situations where access is limited, such as to a wharf, for instance, is the first load ready be delivered as soon as the gates are open? Or do you have to load up first? Why not do that as the last thing for the day? Simply organizing tasks and analyzing performance can help save you time, assets and, in the long run, money.

Improve efficiency of the overall business

An efficient business will increase revenue as a direct and profitable consequence of being efficient. Look at all areas of the business and find ways, in each department, to make it run more efficiently.

Increase capacity on existing trucks

Is your fleet operating at maximum capacities? One of my favorite stories involves a business where every truck in the fleet had a self-loading crane. By operating in pairs, the capacity of half the trucks could be improved simply by removing every second crane.

Monitor loadings and set minimum targets for loads

The real profit from a load usually occurs from the last bit of the load, since each trip incurs a lot of expense and the first part of the load pays for that just to get to breakeven. Have targets to fill the truck, and move heaven and earth to do it wherever possible.

Change the mode

It is easy to get fixated on the way things are currently done and subscribe to the "if it isn't broken, don't fix it" school of thought. It may be that there are better ways of doing the job, using other modes such as long-haul rail, or bulk or palletisation.

Maximize use of backloads

Any dead running is expensive. Obviously, this is occasionally unavoidable because of the specialized nature of transportation work, but in other circumstances it is just lazy. Determine the difference and maximize the use of backloads to decrease the discrepancy.

Increase use of technology in all aspects of the business

If you're not utilizing the latest technology to enhance your bottom line, you are literally cutting your nose off to spite your face! Technology can offer so many benefits, on all fronts in the business. To the extent that it increases efficiencies that is good for the bottom line, if you're not personally comfortable with technology, find someone on your staff who is and charge them with utilizing it to its – and your – maximum efficiency.

Plan smart to reduce penal pay rates

By understanding the exact requirements of the customer, it can often be the case that deadlines are flexible or can be changed. Planning to avoid holiday periods is good practice from a "conflict with the public on clogged roads" point of view and also from a penal pay rates point of view.

Understanding What You Are Doing

Knowing your current fee structure as compared to your current array of offerings, which may have substantially increased since you last updated them, can help you add value, charge more and increase your bottom line profits:

Audit what you are charging to make sure it is all as agreed

Periodically review what you are charging for against what was agreed. It is easy for something to slip between the cracks and become the norm.

For example, one company forgot to charge for returning pallets, even though it was clearly stated in the contract. They eventually reconciled and back-charged, but it should have been picked up sooner and pro-rating services on the back end is never as efficient as simply following the contract to the letter in the first place.

Review what you do for free, and whether that is smart and/or necessary

It is often the case that contracts start off with "limited time only" freebies or one-off situations, which then become the norm. The reason for these can well be lost in the mists of time. Evaluate what you do for free and decide whether that is now appropriate given your current status.

Avoid revenue leakage (e.g. from unauthorized discounts or uncharged activities) and maintain good data

Have checks and balances in place to ensure all is as it should be on the billing end. Make it difficult to issue credits unless they are for genuine reasons. After all, it's easy for disaffected employees to give away credits or undercharge because they think the client deserves it and, without maintaining good data, you might never know the revenue leakage that is occurring under your own nose.

Evaluate profitability routes

Have good information about the profitability of your routes. This often highlights areas where the revenue is less than expected, or does not cover the true cost of the job. Use these facts to justify a price increase.

Customer Ideas

By focusing on the customer, you create a service that can be unmatched by your competitors, gaining you increased revenue by putting the customer first with the following ideas:

Help customers grow their business

By helping your customers grow their own business, the spinoff will be more work for you, and probably means you get more entrenched in their business as a trusted partner. This contributes to repeat business as well as positive word of mouth.

Locate complementary customers to utilize your skills and knowledge, and to fill in gaps in your load profiles

This strategy is about understanding your own skills, and what makes a good customer for you. It may well be that you need a different type of customer to fill in gaps in your load profiles. That makes going out and targeting those types of customers, rather than accepting whoever comes through the door, a priority.

Target the top 20% of customers to build up business, and drop the bottom 20% to make room for them

The 80/20 rule is fascinating. It is the concept that typically 80% of your business comes from 20% of your customers. Mathematically, it is the case that a customer in the top 20% is typically 16 times larger than a customer in the other 80%. In most situations, achieving a small increase in business with a top 20% customer is much easier than trying to do the same with a bottom 20% customer. They are small because that is the way it is. It is generally more productive to try and find more customers like those in your top 20% - so study their characteristics (type of business/ management style / location / etc.) and target more like them. To make room for more top-20%-ers, begin to wean off your bottom 20%.

Get rid of low margin clients and replace with better margin clients

Not all clients are born equal. Study after study shows that a typical business will have a mix of very profitable, and very unprofitable, customers. Do the numbers. Somebody once said there is no point in being a busy fool. In other words, there is no point in having customers that make you little money when doing the same amount of work will result in customers that pay you more. Indeed, your worst customers will often be costing you money if you are truly honest and value your time.

Target driver/customer interaction

Your driver is the public face of your company, out there in the market interacting with customers every day. They see and hear things. They are your primary ambassadors, and the public face of your company. Tap into that knowledge to get a better sense of what clients need so that you and your driver can give it to them in ways your competition can't.

Look at your customer's business and establish needs and requirements

Take time to study your customer's business. Offer to walk around and provide a different set of eyes, i.e. an objective analysis. Often you will be able to offer useful suggestions that the business owner failed to see because her or she is simply too close to the business. It doesn't have to necessarily be about your speciality, but there is inevitably some spinoff when you align yourself with a customer in such a way.

Increase client interaction at all levels to become their preferred supplier

Gain the trust of the customer and be there to help them as often as possible. Use some of the ideas under Question 1 to increase your value to them. This will help you become a preferred supplier, so that they approach you first rather than going to the marketplace and finding someone else less qualified than you.

Increase your customer base

Finally, think about ways to increase your customer base. There are many ways, from advertising to social media to referrals. One simple way to establish your proven brand and appeal to future clients is by asking for testimonials from your former clients – they are easy to get and are very powerful tools when applied prominently.

General

Finally, here are some general tips for how to increase revenue in your existing business:

Advertising

Advertising, both traditional and online, still works. But not all advertising is created equal, nor will all types of advertising be appropriate for your particular business model. Take some time to get creative and find the right types of advertising for you.

Target compatible acquisitions

Rather than growing your own physical assets by buying new equipment, consider growing by absorbing another business. The real value won't necessarily be in their equipment, but will usually be found in their existing customer base. Make sure you have a plan to tap into that before you invest.

Plan!

"Failure to plan is planning to fail," or so goes the old adage. A small amount of planning goes a long way. Discuss your plans with trusted advisors and get their feedback. Get involved in rigorous debates to ensure that every avenue is explored, then work your plant tirelessly to see increased revenue for your trucking and transport business.

Question 3

What If We Don't Have Our Truck Anymore?

What If We Don't Have Our Truck Anymore?

The purpose of this question is to help you think about what it is that your business is really about. Being in transport, we automatically assume that it is the physical truck. However, if you pretend for a moment that you don't have the truck anymore (but can get somebody else to transport your products for you), then you can start thinking laterally about what it is that you really do, or could do, if you broadened your horizons.

This question can really get you thinking about what your core skills are, and the true nature of what it is that you do. The physical act of transporting goods from Point A to Point B might actually be incidental to that activity.

It is a challenging question, and one that you need to refer back to from time to time, no matter how many trucks you may currently have in your fleet.

Service

Can you provide a service other than physical transportation, such as selling your business expertise in transport or being a "connector" to a company with a truck line? Here are some profit-earning tools that exist outside your current vehicle fleet:

Sell your business expertise

If you are a successful business, consider how you might sell those skills to other businesses in your industry. It could range from being on the management board to teaching other, perhaps smaller, companies how to get new clients. It might even be that you earn commissions from new business that is gained.

Become a logistics provider and clip the ticket

It may be that your real asset is your connections in the industry as well as access to good clients. Consider focusing on that and "clipping the ticket" as you pass the physical work on to another provider.

Offer consultancy services

It may be that you work for clients who don't necessarily need your transport, but your wisdom and experience. In this manner you can consult on particular aspects of the business and act as more of a "consultant" based on your industry expertise.

Offer other systems and services, such as forklift hire, secretarial, accounting, HR systems, etc.

If you are well set up with back office support systems, it may be that you can contract to run those services for other companies, while they do the physical world of transporting.

Become a freight forwarder / broker

Instead of offering just transport, offer full logistics services to clients.

Subcontract your services to the client

Offer to run the logistics services on behalf of the client, effectively being part of their team.

Offer de-vanning and related services

This can be a specialist area, and has its own qualifications for bio-security matters.

Become a total transport solution provider: equipment + storage + planning + contracts + partnership + innovation + IT + telemetry + service

Expand the range of your business services to become a full service provider so that your customers don't have to go anywhere else, and others will seek you out because of your broad range of scope and versatility.

Tap into the IT sector

Become a conduit between technology and where the rubber hits the road. Many people shy away from technology, leaving a niche market wide open for those that don't. Implement new technology on behalf of other companies.

Maintain customer relationships, add service/value and outsource

Become the trusted advisor to clients and contract/outsource in the services you need help with so that you are more well-rounded in offerings than the competition.

Contract out for drivers, laborers, etc.

Provide the labor requirements for other companies on a contract basis. Finding good people is getting harder and, when you make it easier, you will find a nice sideline business. For an added bonus, you can also provide driver training as part of the service.

Product

We've covered the services you can offer to increase profits, now let's turn our eyes to which products can best improve your bottom line:

Change your method / mode of transport

Maybe the type of trucks you're currently running is not really the best way to deliver your service. In fact, this whole question is aimed at whether trucks are the essential part of your business or not. If you can change your mode of transport, you might be able to find a better fit in the marketplace.

Convert to owner-driver fleet

There are advantages for and against owner-drivers. It may be that the owner-drivers present you with a much simpler business model and less headaches, since it is in the owner-driver's interest to keep you happy.

Outsource transport to trusted third parties

Rather than shouldering the bulk of the transport burden, consider establishing a relationship(s) with other companies that you trust to do the work on your behalf. Be mindful that you keep the customer relationship with your customer.

Provide truck stop / R & R services

Maybe you have a depot that can be used to provide these services?

Enter into joint ventures / partnerships to share resources and expertise

Consider whether or not you can combine with other similar companies to make the best of your combined skills and expertise. This will double your value to potential customers.

Subcontract the work out

To share the burden and save on various expenses like insurance and overtime, consider employing sub-contractors.

Offer warehousing / storage / hub

Use your business as a distribution hub so that you can combine different types of business, such as a line haul company that needs more efficient local distribution.

Become a MainFreight type operator – i.e. a total transport and logistics provider

MainFreight is a two billion dollar international company that has grown out of a one-truck operation. Read the book about their story, *Ready, Fire, Aim* by Keith Davis (Random House New Zealand, 2013) and consider what lessons there are for you within this unparalleled success story.

Other

Finally, there is one more option that may or may not be right for you:

Retire and re-deploy your assets!

Review your business, how it makes you feel, what it earns for you, the headaches and success, the failures or frustrations. Is it worth continuing in its present state? Or you up for a major overhaul or restructure? If not, it might be more profitable to sell out, invest the money and take life more easily!

Question 4

How Can I Increase My Effective Prices by Just 5%?

Question 4

How Can I Increase My Effective Prices by Just 5%?

For many companies, a 5% increase in prices -- or revenue from the same level of activity -- would double or even triple the bottom line result, because any price increase effectively falls straight to the bottom line as pure profit.

But price increases don't necessarily need to be the headline here. Just like McDonalds, who asks "Would you like fries with that?" in an effort to "chip away" at profits one add-on order at a time, success is ultimately about the total amount of money you generate from each trip that matters. So, effective prices increases can come from a variety of sources:

Capacity utilization

How you utilize the capacity of your trucks on each trip – efficiently, wisely, creatively – can dramatically increase your potential profits:

Increase utilization of capacity

At the first port of call, make sure the truck is full to maximize capacity.

Maximize full back-loads

Wherever there is a dead load, ask the question, "What can I be using this space for?" Even marginal pricing will generate revenue. The point is that the costs of the trip will already be incurred, so any extra revenue falls straight to the bottom line, even if it formally seemed insignificant.

Preplanning for more efficiency

Plan the loads as far ahead of time as possible, so that you have time to fill in any gaps in the load as the trip approaches.

Charging Basis

Pricing is an issue, and when you charge effectively – based on sound business practices and added value – it can increase your prices by 5% - or more:

Change your method of charging

Inevitably what you are currently charging will be based on history, because that is the way it has always been done. Stand back and think about whether that is really the best pricing option for where you are as a company today. In some cases, it may be more efficient to convert bulk loads into palletized cargo for easier handling, and in other cases the opposite may be true. A change in basis can be an avenue to change the effective pricing.

Implement new technology to do the work for you

New technology may provide a better way of achieving your goals: faster, easier, and even cheaper. Any of these benefits has the potential to increase effective revenue (i.e. dollars per distance).

Methodology – check on how pricing is done and identify better ways to achieve the goal

Review how you price, and whether it is a fair reflection of what you actually do in your current capacity (see historical pricing, above). Circumstances change over time, so make sure that your pricing model keeps up with your current level of service.

Increase the value of service add-ons, such as IT, documentation, etc.

Again, review the actual services currently provided and consider whether any of these could/should include add-on services and out of pocket charges. (Look to other industries for numerous examples.)

Add recognizable value between your customer and their customer, which adds value to your customer's brand

You are often the public face of your client, both to the public at large and your customer's customer. If you can demonstrate that you add value to them, consider how you can specifically charge for that.

Help customers reduce overall transport costs

By better understanding what your customer does, you may be able to save them costs and improve your own charges. For example, one warehouse operator noticed bulk goods going out to be bagged and then returned to the same store, so they bought bagging equipment to do it on site. This simple act saved their customer transport costs and became a new source of revenue for them.

Reduce inefficiencies and revenue slippage

Audit your current billing process and know exactly what you are – and are not – charging for, and whether that is appropriate.

Have a written contract that specifies exactly what the service is, including routes, delivery points, etc.

By having a written contract, it is easy to set out exactly what services you are providing and where you are charging for them, to avoid conflicts later. This reduces the chances of doing work that you ought to, but are not, being paid for. It also means that you can be specific about how you do the service. One example is the route that you follow. If that route is out of action, say following a massive landslip, then it gives you the start point to re-negotiate the contract. Finally, a written contract enables you to be specific about where the service stops, so that any extra services – i.e. "scope creep" – are clearly an extension to the contract.

Invest in technology and share the benefits (and cost) with clients

New technology can be expensive, but offer big savings in the long run (i.e. maximizing efficiency, paperwork, ease of service, etc.). Consider how these costs – and rewards – can be shared to reduce risks, and also lock in the client to using you.

Check accuracy of charging

Audit what you are charging. Make sure it is based on facts, and not assumptions that have been passed down from time immemorial (i.e. historic pricing). Circumstances change; so should your prices.

Prices

Altering your prices just a little can have significant effects on bottom-line profits. There are probably a variety of ways that you can increase pricing fairly, and probably should have done so long ago:

Include annual inflation clauses to contracts

Having a written contract makes it easier to have "event reviews" to account for annual inflation. This can include, for example, increasing annual pricing by at least the CPI, and having specific review dates.

Increase prices often, but in small amounts

Implementing small changes more often can help to keep the issue below the radar and of small consequence to the client.

Charge for changes in items that are beyond your control

Unless you are a good gambler, why should you take the risk – and overage – on things beyond your control? Have provisions in your contact to on-charge items that are beyond your control such as fuel, Road User Charges (RUC's), government charges, road tolls and the like.

Have service level agreements (SLA) with clients, which includes what is expected of them

A SLA provides the basis to set out the expectations of both parties. If they are not performing, it provides a basis to renegotiate. For example, if performance of your service requires a forklift to load the vehicle, then note that the client will provide it in a timely manner to avoid you incurring downtime and losing revenue opportunities because the vehicle is otherwise tied up waiting for the promised equipment.

Identify clients that don't focus solely on price, and tailor service to their needs

While the perception is that "price is all that matters," it has been said the price is only the fifth most important issue to a client, and that six out of seven people prefer to buy on value. Identify those customers and tailor your service to those people who will pay more rather than those who focus solely on price – and who assume "lower is better".

Promote sustainable pricing as the key to your value proposition

It is usually in your clients' best interests to have a reliable business partner. You need to make a profit to make that happen, at least over the longer term. Your prices should reflect a sustainable business model.

Diversify into areas that support your pricing structure

Review what you do, do well and do most often. It may be that you are better at some types of work than others. It may be that your business is set up in a particular way (e.g. quality gear) that means you should focus on particular markets that can support that business model.

Offer greater flexibility to justify higher prices

Providing adaptability and flexibility can impose costs on your business, either as additional costs or loss of revenue. However, if that can be adequately compensated for, then it is a worthwhile idea to pursue. A small additional cost from you may be small change in terms of the potential benefits to the client.

Collect cash as early as possible

It is always a good business practice to collect cash as soon as possible. It takes a lot to cover bad debts. Offer alternate forms of payment. It is true that credit card fees are a cost, but in the grand scheme of things such minor fees can be a small price to pay if it becomes the only way you can *get* paid. In short, don't get sucked into majoring in things that don't matter.

Charge for *all* incidentals

Review whether these are part of the core service or should be "extras," but in either event mark them clearly and charge accordingly.

Offer premium services, such as priority service or guaranteed time of delivery, and charge accordingly

In almost all markets, there is room for premium services. As a consumer you are faced with this everyday: business or cattle class seats on an airplane, upmarket and down market clothes stores, by-pass lanes at fairground attractions, special seats in the movies, etc. There is clearly a demand for premium services. It may be priority pick-up times, guaranteed delivery times, particular drivers. What is it for you customers? Find out and charge accordingly.

Recognizable service / branding value

Has your service been documented? Are there core values for your company that you could communicate to clients? Never underestimate the power of branding when it comes to increasing your price points.

Reinforce value added through Key Performance Indicators (KPIs)

Are there some Key Performance Indicators (KPI's) that you can use to sell the "value" of your service? Such as... on-time deliveries, low level of breakages, driver performance, number of trained staff? If so, identify, then charge for them.

Quantify the opportunity cost and hassle of changing providers

It is easy for a client to say that they will change suppliers if you don't pull your prices into line. Often, however, this is a hollow threat. Think about the relationship you have with your client: time, knowledge of their business, knowing the quirks, flexibility of service and so forth. These take a long time to establish, and are hard to replace quickly. There are also risks in changing. We hear examples on the news all the time. Payroll systems that don't work, relocations that don't work, the list goes on. Use these arguments to justify keeping the relationship going and then, by all means, get the service in line with the client's expectations.

General rate increase and regular reviews

Think of increasing prices as process, one that takes time. Bite it off in small pieces and take it slowly but methodically.

General

As always, there are a variety of ways "in general" for you to increase price that aren't based solely on price:

Know the facts and justify value

There is nothing that beats knowing the facts. Have a system that tracks the revenues and costs of particular tasks and/or customers. This will identify areas where you are undercharging, and also give you ammunition to justify prices if the client questions them. When the true costs of providing a product or servicing a customer are known it can be eye-opening – things always come out of the woodwork. Additional costs, loads less than guaranteed, etc. In this case, knowledge really is the foundation of increased profit.

Know the facts and identify where there is slippage

It's been said before but worth repeating: excessive waiting times, incorrect charging basis, loads not at levels you quoted on, etc. These can all cause slippage and result in increased work, time and resources allocated without the basis for additional charges, i.e. lost profit.

Communicate with customer in person

There is nothing like the personal touch to increase your value to the customer at no cost to you or the organization.

Implement transparency

Be transparent in your dealings with customers and staff. You don't have to give away your trade secrets, but being excessively private and "secret squirrel" stuff is overrated and, frankly, unnecessary. Most people don't care, and in any event they have their own problems. But sharing information creates trust, and it enables you to show that, for instance, a certain activity is simply not paying its way under the current arrangement.

Audit rates/charges frequently

It's easy to get into bad habits and overlook key issues that could either add to profits or are draining them. Keep a watching brief and use common sense as to whether something is right or wrong.

Look at the whole-of-life cost to the customer

It's generally hard to get new customers on board. Think about the lifetime value that they represent. Some will be worth the effort of investing in, some won't. Focus on those that represent the best return for your time and effort and make them a priority.

Deliver contract in person

There is nothing like the personal touch and to eyeball a client as you sign a contract. You will get a lot of non-verbal feedback as to how the client really feels about the contract and/or your services, which can be helpful not in just serving them in the future, but other customers as well.

Understand and control costs

Think of profit differently. After all, a dollar saved is the same as a dollar of extra revenue. So, within reason, finding ways to budget and save money is a worthwhile activity. But do not get obsessively bogged down. There is usually more upside to focusing on revenue than costs. I like the analogy of putting a golf ball to help put this in focus: if you don't hit hard enough it will never go in the hole on the first shot, even if you repeat the shot 1 million times. But hit it hard enough to reach the hole, and sometimes, just sometimes, it will go in. Focusing on reducing cost targets, which even if you achieved them would not solve the problem, is not as smart as having a consistent game.

Rank customers and eliminate the bottom tier

Rank customers according to various criteria and eliminate the bottom tiers. This can include profitability, complainers, value buyers, prospects for growth, in your target market.

Invest in technology

Keep up with the play. At some time you will be faced with a competitor that does, and you don't want to be out-modernized.

Question 5

Know the Numbers – What Better Decisions Could You Make?

Question 5

Know the Numbers - What Better Decisions Could You Make?

There is no substitute for knowing exactly what is happening in your business.

As my good friend and the author of *Pricing for Profit* (AMACOM, 2009), Dale Furtwengler, said, "Ignorance is not bliss... it is expensive"

Have good information and suddenly new possibilities to run your business more profitably will emerge. Think of areas where you can have better information, and what you would do with that information.

Oftentimes, it is not the actual numbers that really matter, but the process involved in finding them. The fact that you are thinking about an issue in a structured way is a tremendous start.

So don't be put off because you think it is all about accountants having to provide reams and reams of data. In fact, that can be worse. Rather, some very simple measures are often more effective, including the following:

Products and Capacity

Being on top of what products you offer as well as the kind of capacity you can manage will help you bid more effectively:

Know the best freight mix so you can maximize revenues and, more importantly, profit

Inevitably you have a range of products and services – different types of freight, different destinations, different client types. Fully understand the profitability of each to maximise bottom line profits.

Identify leakage so you can charge for everything that has been done

Know the right numbers to challenge whether you are charging for all activity undertaken.

Know the usable space / capacity of every truck in your fleet so you can fill it by targeting specific customers

Maximizing utilization is most likely to lead to maximum profits. Know where the holes are and target customers who provide that type of freight so that every load can be as full, and as profitable, as possible.

Know what you are selling so you know what is left, i.e. "top stow"

Fully understand both the weight and volume of what your carry. Consider what low weight, high volume products for top stow would work, if that is relevant.

Utilize your assets so that they are being used in the most productive way

Understand how your assets are being used, and if that is the most productive use for them.

Know the right vehicle for the job

Understand what the job entails, and your vehicle capabilities to ensure there is a good match. After all, there's no point using a big V8 around town when a puddle jumper will do the job.

Know the true returns from each part of the business and consider sharing business with traditional opposition to maximize returns

Know the areas of key profitability so you can find the holes that aren't meeting expectations. Consider how you can combine forces with other players to increase the overall profitability: i.e. where 1 + 1 = 3.

Clients

Know your clients and you are likely to discover key ways to please, satisfy and influence them for increased satisfaction and profits:

Understand more about the customer's business and encourage customer growth

Know the customer's business so well that you can identify where the opportunities lie for growth. After all, growth for them will inevitably be good for you.

Know where the client demand is so you can cater for it

Understand your wider business environment, so that you know where potential growth options will be coming from.

Identify A-list clients and focus on them, change the service for B and C-list clients

Accept the fact that you will have A-, B- and C-List clients: all businesses do. Focus on the "A" clients, and consider changing the level of service the B's and C's.

Target your top 20% clients to increase profitability

Your top 20% of clients are the ones you should target: they are usually better all around, and have the most potential. It is generally easier to move top clients to great performers than move low performers to average performers.

Know the client's business so you have the ability to commit and gain leverage from long term contracts

Understand how you can add long-term value to clients and put long-term contracts in place that enable you to do that, with a win-win situation for you *and* the client.

Financial

Dollars are often found looking for pennies. In other words, knowing your financial situation – the good, the bad and the ugly – can help you focus on profits while dodging dead weight:

Know the running costs for your vehicles so these can be monitored closely

Know what it costs to run each vehicle/fleet and make better decisions on when to replace them. Also use this information to use the most efficient vehicles first, and retire the most expensive vehicles when there is a downturn in activity.

Know the cost of incidentals and decide whether these should be charged and, if so, that the costs are reasonable

Know the information, and you are 90% on the way to making the correct decision.

Justify rate increases

Know the facts and you can use that information to justify price increases.

Eliminate low profit clients / jobs

Know the profitability of each job so you can eliminate the least profitable clients to focus on the more

profitable clients (we all have them). All businesses have products, services and customers that are not profitable – often they just don't want to own up to it.

Know the key performance indicators (KPIs) on the vital parts of the business

Have KPI's that reflect on the true items and issues that you can change manage in the business.

Know the most profitable parts of your business and grow those

Know profitability by activity so that you can focus on those parts where you can achieve higher profitability.

Know the profitability of each client, focus on them and find more like them

Use your profitability per client and general understanding of your clients to find more of the type that you want.

Know the true cost of ownership, and whether an owner-driver situation is best

Know the true cost of owning your own fleet, including management time, to decide whether owner-drivers are more – or less – profitable for you.

Know the numbers so you can do smarter / more accurate quoting

The best time to get the price right is the first time you quote for the business. As we all know it's a lot harder to go back and change later. Therefore, have good information available before you quote.

Know department / branch revenues and costs, and make the manager accountable

Delegate authority and responsibility, and make people accountable for varying degrees of loss and profit – otherwise they'll be responsible for neither.

Let bad payers go and free up time and money for more productive uses

It is easy to get sucked in by customers who don't pay on time and question everything. Know who they are and avoid them where possible, or change the terms of service. In other words, make bad payers cash before delivery. They won't like it, but you are far better off dealing with new business prospects that will add to your business rather than dealing with issues for which there is no return.

Identify cost increases early so these can be passed on without incident

Scan your environment and be aware of what is happening. Letting customers know well ahead of time what is happening is much more palatable, and enables them to make their own adjustments. Springing price changes on them at the last minute is not a smart move.

Operations

Knowing the nuts and bolts of your physical operations – on the ground, in the garage and on the road – will help identify areas to reduce loss and increase price:

Review claims to detect performance issues

Review your claims and it will tell you a lot about the business. This includes performance issues (such as damaged goods) and whether you are pushing the boundaries pricewise.

Review damage to detect poor performance

Review vehicle damage to understand how your gear is being treated. This will help prevent costly damage and improve performance.

Plan maintenance to provide less downtime

Understand the maintenance requirements of your gear and factor that into your routines to ensure you have maximum uptime.

Institute a vehicle replacement policy to ensure your fleet is fit for purpose

Understand the requirements of your work and equipment so that you have the best fit for the job.

Where it not necessary, don't run on public holidays to reduce risk of accidents and to not incur penal rates

Know what deliveries have time constraints and which don't, so that you minimize running on public holidays when there are both added costs (labor rates) and higher chances of accidents with clogged roads.

Monitor driver behavior and routes to ensure efficient operation, and that they are doing what they are supposed to be doing

Understand whether drivers are following your proscribed routes and taking the required breaks, and have protocols in place for when/if they are not.

Use "real time" data to make better decisions on the move

Where possible, collect real time data and make changes as you go that will save you money – and increase profit.

Talk to drivers to find out where the opportunities are

Your drivers have ears in the market, both with customers and competitors. They hear things you might not, so utilize that knowledge.

Measure productivity by truck so your most efficient trucks are used for the job

It goes without saying that you should use the most efficient equipment to maximize profits and repair/improve the rest of the fleet so they can maximize their capacity as well.

Look at taking over runs that other people are avoiding because they don't fully understand the issues

Understand the issues and get good at solving problems. There is money to be made where others fear to tread, often because they don't have the confidence of understanding what is happening.

Know the gaps in the business that need your attention

Focus your energy where it matters most. Have the confidence to major in the majors, and let other people worry about the minor things.

Know turnaround times so you can recover hidden costs loading and unloading

Your business is not making money when the equipment is idle. Low cost airlines have found may ways of speeding up the process. So can you.

Know the quiet times, so that repair and maintenance can be done at that time to maximize revenue capability

Plan for maintenance at times that don't interfere with your normal business operating hours. More and more it is the case that service providers will work around your requirements, i.e. servicing trucks during the night or before the work day begins.

Understand the true returns from investments in IT and pursue them when appropriate

Do your homework when it comes to technology and understand what it can do for you. Many people only use a small part of their available technology, thus reducing the opportunity to increase their profits.

Identify lost hours and charge out

Monitor driver hours and understand if there are consistent losses due to issues beyond your control, such as clients not doing what they undertook to do. Charge where necessary.

Identify opportunities from a High Productivity Motor Vehicle (HPMV) standpoint and use them to improve efficiency

Understand changes to the road rules and understand where you can benefit. Don't give all the benefits back to the customer when you can reap some for yourself.

Undertake staff performance assessments and up-skill

Understand the skills in your workforce. Often the last time you considered these skills was on a review of their resume, but do a regular review to ensure that you are using your people to their maximum potential.

Future planning

Take time out to think about the future. Get away, shoot the breeze and take time to put life – and business – in perspective.

Question 6

What Changes in the Environment Will Impact on Your Business in the Next Two Years?

Question 6

What Changes in the Environment Will Impact on Your Business in the Next Two Years?

Change is inevitable; it's also welcome. Change brings with it opportunities for those that are quick on their feet, and disaster for those that don't adapt!

Use the following checklist of ideas to decide how your business will be placed to meet the (inevitable) future. Some of these ideas will be more important in your current business model than others, but peruse them all to take what you can and let the others marinate. You never know when a current business model will change and allow for future progress. Think about each idea raised and how it might affect your business. Ask yourself the question, "What can I do about it?"

With so much change, one simple solution might be to have contracts that allow flexibility to adapt to changing conditions, such as new charges, without creating issues on both sides.

Operations

How can your operations change for the better? That is the focus of the following solutions for driving increased profits:

New health and safety rules will involve potentially massive change. Are you prepared?

This is somewhat self-explanatory. The changes will be significant. Are you ready to implement them? Will it involve a change in the way you deal with your client(s)? Will it involve extra cost(s) that you need to recover? Does your existing contract allow you to do this? Do you even have an existing contract? Answering these questions will put you in good stead for when change does inevitably come.

The increase in fossil fuel prices is a constant

The pressure of finding affordable fossil fuel, and charging accordingly, is still on. The volatility has gone for the present, but it is costing more and more to search for, and produce, oil. How will you handle the ongoing and future changes in this market?

Dealing with the aging driver pool

Currently, the average driver is 54 years old. This statistic is alarming. What implications does it have for your business? What does it mean in terms of ability to do the job, especially where lifting and physical effort is required?

Facing a potential driver shortage

This is a looming issue. How are you placed to compete for a skill shortage? Can your business support higher wages? Can your business support I shortage of labour? Do you need to invest in new technologies?

Customers' operating business models are constantly changing

Your customers are constantly changing to meet the demands of their marketplace. How are you placed to help your customers? What will the changes look like?

VDAM (Vehicle Dimension and Mass) rules

Theoretically, this allows for more efficiency. But will it, really? And what will it mean to your business?

Expectations are changing – what is the Road Transport image now? And what do you need to do to improve it?

Society's standards and expectations change over time. What is the current image of the Road Transport industry? How does this impact your customers? How does it reflect on your ability to employ new staff? What does it mean about business practices that you used in the past? Facing the future – and the facts about changing public perception – will help you deal with both.

Expectations are changing as to what are considered appropriate working conditions, and a push for more work-life balance

What are your working conditions like? How do you treat your staff? Do these need to change to meet the new expectations? What will it mean on the way you run your business?

Limited availability of skilled workforce

On top of driver shortages, there may well be overall skill shortages as well. How do you plan to overcome this? What will it mean to your company?

Potential rail impact for containers and inland wharves

Is a resurgent rail network a threat to you? Or can you use it to your advantage by appealing to clients who can respect the dependability of road transportation?

Increasing compliance costs in many parts of the business

Compliance is increasing in all aspects of the business world. How does it affect your business? Will you embrace it, challenge it or ignore it?

Financial

There are always more financial aspects to consider, and here are some of our more pressing issues at present:

Exchange rates – examining their impact on capital costs and client profitability

If exchange rates trend downward, it will increase the cost of replacing your equipment, so you will need more money – or friendly lenders. Conversely, it may make your customers more profitable and less averse to price increases.

Interest rates are likely to rise

How is your business placed if interest rates rise? What actions can you take now to reduce the impact?

Consider the possibility of regional taxes – how will that affect your charge outs? Can you on-charge?

If regional taxes are implemented, can you recover these from your client?

Increasing rail ferry costs

If your work covers both islands, are you protected if the ferry charge increases to cover the recent misfortunes that have plagued the ferries?

Increasing competition for drivers and increasing pressure on wage costs

There is increasing pressure from an expanding economy for the labor resource you need to drive your trucks. How are you placed to counter this?

Prepare as industries go through cycles

The Dairy industry has been on a high and is now retreating rapidly. How will that affect you, as demand weakens and customers close the proverbial checkbook? What about other lesser known industries? Keep abreast of what is happening in your market segment and consider what impact it might have on you. Being prepared can make a big difference while your less compared competitors drown in your wake.

Technology

Staying abreast of technology will help you maximized profits by increasing efficiency in the organization and attracting tech-savvy customers who appreciate your modernization efforts:

Rapidly changing technology

It is a given that technology has, and will continue to, change at a rapid pace. How do you, as a company, plan to keep on top of these changes? How will you decide what is right for you? How will you finance it? What, if anything, are your competitors doing about? Who are you real competitors? Remember, it may not be other trucking companies.

Online business including bookings will increase

How do you use on-line technology now? How do customers interact with you? Track and trace is now a big issue - how are you placed to take advantage of it?

Toll roads may increase. Can you on-charge the cost?

There is talk of new toll roads In the offing. What will this mean to your business model? Can you on-charge the costs?

More technological policing is coming

The new technologies are pervasive. As a result, it will be harder to pull the wool over the authority's eyes. How will it affect your business with GPS tracking and e-log books for example?

Technology advancements in all aspects of your business, from truck operational management to accounting systems

Not only is the speed of change continuing, the width and breadth is also changing. How will it affect your business? How will you keep up?

Environment

There are factors outside of your control that affect pricing, charging and costs. How you respond to them will make the difference in your bottom line:

Waste management / handling issues are increasingly public issues

There is certainly a move to more public concern and scrutiny at the whole issue of waste management. It could well include vehicles that emit plumes of black smoke. Where does your business sit in relation to this? Are you prepared to make your trucks more ecologically efficient, or pay the consequences?

Environmental issues that may be affecting your clients, i.e. dairy and waterways pollution

The same concerns may be held about your clients. Dairy farming is a topical issue. Is there an issue of guilt by association? How can you help your clients achieve their goals efficiently, and ecologically? In all aspects of your business, think of ways to be a solution, not a problem.

Extreme weather events seem to be occurring more often

Extreme weather events are more widely publicized nowadays. Is there a trend occurring? How does weather affect your business? How can you put your client's minds at ease that your trucks can weather any such condition?

Improvements in road infrastructure do happen. How can you exploit that?

Along with the publicized impending congestion issue, there are in fact positive changes happening. How can you benefit from the new infrastructure? How can you associate this good news with more/better business?

Potential change in government policies

There is always a risk that a new government is elected and policies are changed. What are the risks to your business? What are the upsides? Whenever possible, develop a talent for "spinning" news to your advantage.

Increasing emission standards

Increasing emission standards are a fact or life. How does it affect your business? Capital investment, operating procedures, client concerns, client demands?

More traffic congestion

Certain parts of the network will come under increasing pressure. Does this mean that your business hours will change as you hit the road earlier and earlier to avoid congestion? What does it mean about your ability to meet client demands for on-time performance? Will your workday change?

Will the Consumer Guarantees Act affect you?

Do the increasingly stringent consumer protection laws affect your business? Do you deal with the public? Again, how can you turn these issues into plus-signs in your profit column?

Bio diesel may be a fuel for the future

Are there any issues with the new fuels? If so, how can you inform your customer about them so that you appear more knowledgeable than the competition?

Question 7

How Do I Run the Company?

How Do I Run the Company?

How you run the company – i.e. the day to day operations – can have a significant impact on both your and your staff's performance, and ultimately the very profitability of the business itself.

Your business should be run in a professional, business-like manner that is as efficient, and profit-producing, as possible. The ideas listed below are techniques that can help you run a cleaner, tighter, better ship.

The overriding advice is from a person called Michael Gerber, author of *The E-Myth Revisited* (HarperCollins, 2009), who explains how you need to work *on* the business, and not *in* it:

Staff

Your people are not only your #1 asset but learning how to delegate, manage and lead will definitely help you to work on the business, rather than it, increasing profit at the same time:

Provide for staff input and involvement at all levels

Harness the power of the collective workforce by tapping into it in a real and meaningful way. You do not have a monopoly on good ideas, so provide for staff input and involvement at all levels, including creative solutions to ongoing problems.

Provide for feedback avenues

Employee ideas can often fall on deaf ears if there are no lanes open for them to provide open and honest communication. Provide the means by which employees can provide feedback and be open to challenges.

Identify core values

Identify what it is that your company stands for. These don't have to be idealistic – it can be as simple as maintaining a tidy and clean fleet.

Remain open to new ideas

No matter how "right" you believe you are, always be open to new voices, perspectives and, above all, ideas. You may be surprised how much your employees are thinking about the business as they go about their lives.

Provide incentives

Incentives recognize participation and reward staff in ways that are appreciated by the entire company. They don't have to be large, elaborate or expensive, as the kudos can in itself be a major motivator.

Plan for weekly one-on-one meetings with staff

It is often a good practice to have structured one-on-one time with the staff to nip issues in the bud and develop effective work plans and targets for the coming week.

Promote open communication throughout organization

With modern technology, communication is easier than ever. A weekly email or YouTube video is quick to prepare and a powerful motivator for your staff and management.

Promote regular staff appraisals

Review staff performance regularly to ensure that they know you're not only watching but interested in their performance, future and growth.

Use well trained staff

There is a famous quote, which goes along the lines of, "What say I train my staff and they leave," to which the answer is, "What say you don't train them and they stay?". In other words, employ people that are smarter than you.

Pay a fair price for the right people

People (staff) can make or break your business. Don't penny pinch by hiring the lowest bidder instead of the most talented; they can repay your loyalty many times over.

Management

Succession planning

What are you doing about succession planning? Should members of the family automatically get the top roles? Or should merit be in the mix as well? What training are you giving people to step up to the next level?

Pay yourself a wage to ensure cost is built into the business

It is tempting to leave your wages out of the books and great as part of the bottom line. This is false economy. The business should stand on its own feet. If forces you to take into accounting the true cost of running the business, and it separates out the investment from your labor. If you don't pay yourself a wage because the business can't afford it, that suggests there is a problem to address. So ask yourself, is there?

Flat hierarchy

Do you operate a flat hierarchy, or is the business top heavy?

Lean and mean

There is something to be said for lean and mean organizations, so ask yourself, "Where does your business sit – lean and mean or fat and bloated?"

Organize formal weekly senior management meetings

Successful businesses tend to have a structured approach with formal meetings. That doesn't mean they are stuffy or long winded. In fact, they can be quite the opposite. They are a powerful tool to provide cohesion to the business and ensure the business is on the right path.

Delegate early to good staff

Delegate more authority to good people sooner rather than later – they will relish the challenge, and mostly they swim rather than sink to the bottom.

Mentor your staff

Support their growth through mentorship and have goal of them taking over your role, so you can be released to do bigger and better things yourself.

Governance

Keeping an eye on the organizational side of your business through strong governance will free you up for higher level thinking and decision making:

Use professional advisors (accountants / lawyers/ bankers) in the business

Make use of external advisors to challenge yourself and justify your decisions. These people have wide and diverse experience to tap into and take advantage of.

Conduct regular meetings with funders

Keep your funders involved. It is a good discipline, and makes it a lot easier when you need help in difficult times or, in better times, need additional funding to expand.

Have a Management Board to challenge your decisions

Make use of a Management Board, whose focus should be on how the business is performing as well as strategy. It is less formal than a Board of Directors and there are less legal issues. Pick people that will challenge you and, for optimum effectiveness, meet at least monthly.

Hold formal regular (monthly preferably) board meetings

Whether you have a Board of Directors or Management Board, meet regularly and make yourself accountable to the group.

Run a business, not a lifestyle

Don't confuse the issues. The business may indeed support your lifestyle, but run it like a true business. If you haven't got the time or enthusiasm anymore, delegate to somebody who has.

Run your company with integrity, clear direction and a mission statement

Have clear goals for your business, and run it with integrity.

Have a five-year strategy

Think about the future often – what will change in the environment? How will I change? What opportunities are appearing? Can I make used of those?

Skills

Skills are often the great equalizer between yourself and the competition, so keep up with yours to ensure that you and your organization are always out front:

Ensure the company learns how to use new technology

Most technology is underused. The best approach may not be the shiny new object, but learning how to use the old one better.

Outsource training

Consider using outside providers to train your people on new and emerging skills sets.

In-house trainer

In some cases a dedicated in-house trainer may be the best solution to ensure that training is constant, updated and thorough.

Offer staff training in areas outside the straight technical

Consider training staff in areas not necessarily related to their jobs. It boosts their self-esteem and their interest in helping the organization grow.

Operations

Maintaining effective and productive operations will help the company run more smoothly on all levels:

Maintain minimal overheads

Operate with minimal overheads to ensure the company runs lean.

Set high standards in fleet presentation

Set high standards to create good impressions all round: with the public, the client, the staff who take pride in the business and keep the gear operating well.

Undertake customer surveys

Challenge yourself to see what customers really think about your service. It can certainly bring you back to earth, but the business will be better for it.

Have operationally sound practices

Operate the business with integrity and use sound practices. Short cuts inevitably catch you out and bite you in the behind.

Identify high performance of staff and customers

Identify and reinforce high performers with more rewards, authority and new challenges.

Remain open to change

Be open to new ways of doing things across the board: in operations, with technology, with staff ideas and leaving your comfort zone in the rear view mirror.

Financial

Staying on top of the company's finances will help you see where there are opportunities and challenges, both of which can lead to more profit when approached directly:

Know the profitability of the company at all times

There is no excuse for not knowing how the business is operating. It gives you control and confidence.

Benchmark with other companies

Find similar companies and offer to benchmark progress with them. The idea – and the challenge – here is to change your perspective and see what is possible.

Implement daily and weekly reporting

Implement at least weekly reporting and, where relevant, daily reporting. Use week-on-week and year-on-year comparisons to make sure you are progressing,

Use IT to get timely numbers

Make use of IT to get up to date, relevant numbers.

Prepare budgets

Plan your business budget carefully and set targets to achieve.

Monitor each project

Constantly review the key accounts and sectors in your business.

Monitor KPI's and ensure that you and the staff understand what they mean

Identify key KPI's and make sure that everybody understands what they measure, and why they are measured. Perhaps the most famous KPI was at British Airways, where if a plane was late taking off by a certain number of minutes, it was reported to the CEO.

Transparency within business as to performance

Be open about the company's performance. Make it easy to raise issues where there are problems, rather than leaving them to be "discovered" when a real issue arises.

Have strong debtor control

Maintain strong debtor and cash controls.

Separate cost and profit centers

Segment the business and keep different profit centers, to truly understand where the business is doing well and not so well.

Business Development

Develop the business to keep it growing, evolving, changing, improving and, above all, out-earning your expectations:

Brainstorm with local businesses

Consider brainstorming issues with other local businesses, not necessarily in the same industry. Outside perspectives can be interesting and insightful.

Join relevant industry and business groups

Make use of local business groups and attend industry conferences to keep up with the latest emerging developments and use them to enhance and grow your business.

Final Comment

So, that's the list. You are now armed with something in the order of 275 ideas on how to improve your profits. Most of them are common sense, and many may not suit your particular business. However, if even just a few ideas *do* fit, they could pay a big dividend to you – and the more ideas you implement, the higher your chances of reaping bigger profits.

Begin the process by selecting a few of them that make sense to you and pursue those first. Discuss them with your trusted advisors, with your staff, with your customers and anybody else interested in your business. Start from the point of view that they *can* work, and see where you get to.

The ultimate goal is to make more profit. This book has tried to focus you on looking at the bigger picture. While we need to keep an eye on costs, the business will only expand when we take a wider, worldview and look at the company with a new, unique and sometimes challenging perspective. Put yourself in the driver's seat on that train and see a new horizon. These ideas provide you with an opportunity to do just that.

Enjoy the journey.

If you need help, please don't hesitate to contact me: Geoff Vautier

+64 212 459014

geoff@howtoincreaseprices.com

About the Author

Geoff Vautier is an international speaker, consultant and entrepreneur. His professional background in New Zealand was, for over 30 years, as a Chief Financial Officer in industries very much at the coalface of the physical economy: trucking, meat processing, and retail.

That work as a CFO focused very much on understanding how businesses worked, and telling the story, so that managers could make better decisions. Through both his professional work and personal pursuits, Geoff has developed an interest in pricing – after all, prices play a major role in determining your profit!

As a result of this work, Geoff published a book called *How to Increase Prices: Seven Simple Steps to Make it Happen and Keep the Customer.* See www.howtoinreaseprices.com to purchase your copy. He regularly presents course on such topics as:

• How to discover the nuggets of gold buried in your business;

• Excel Secrets for busy people;

• How to increase price and keep the customer happy;

• How to complete you accounts by day 3 or less.

There is a common theme through all of this – and his other work, which is practical information to make businesses work better. He has implemented many weekly reporting systems across many industries, which focus on how the business is performing, and what can be done better.

If you have any question on the material presented in this book, talk to him – he may well have a solution for you.

Contact Geoff on Geoff@howtoincreaseprices.com

++ 64 212 459014

SPEAKING • PROJECT MANAGEMENT • CONSULTING

How to Increase Prices Boot Camp

What is it?

A six-week training program that will give you the confidence to raise your prices and make them stick.

What do I get?

The package consists of:

- ✓ A physical copy of the book **How to Increase Prices:** Seven Simple Steps to Make it Happen and Keep the Customer;
- ✓ An electronic copy of the book to read on your e-book reader;
- ✓ 9 YouTube videos (140-minutes running time) covering each of the seven steps, together with an introduction and summary;
- ✓ A physical copy of the workbook (125 pages) that has supporting exercises for each of the videos;
- ✓ An electronic copy of the workbook;
- ✓ 30 Special reports;
- ✓ PLUS a special bonus for RTF attendees – a half-hour telephone consultation on any aspect of the course.

How does it work?

You register and pay for the program. You will then receive a copy of the book and the workbook in the mail. Every four days you will receive an email with a link to the new video, which you can watch at your leisure, and then answer questions in the workbook. In between these videos, you will receive Special Reports on a wide range of topics related to pricing.

What are the seven key steps to increasing my prices?

1. Learn to have confidence in the value of what you are selling;
2. Know exactly what it is that you are selling;
3. Know exactly what it is that the buyer is actually buying;
4. Know the numbers;
5. Increase your prices;
6. Do the deed – tell your customers;
7. Make the cash stick.

Why should I buy?

Because pricing is one of the most important activities in your business, the extra money goes straight onto your bottom line. Imagine what even just a 1% increase in prices would do?

If this program helps you increase prices by just a fraction more than you would otherwise have done, it will have been absolutely worth its weight in gold.

How to do I order?

Talk to Geoff on +(64) 212 459014 or send an email to geoff@howtoincreaseprices.com

Order from:

http://www.howtoincreaseprices.com/increase-prices-self-study-program

Made in the USA
Las Vegas, NV
24 September 2023

78098447R00057